SING
GLORIA

A JOURNEY *to* ADVENT

Created by DAVE CLARK

Arranged & Orchestrated by PHIL NITZ

PUBLISHING COMPANY

lillenas.com

Contents

Carol Medley

includes
Sing, Sing, Sing
Angels, from the Realms of Glory
Hark! the Herald Angels Sing
Angels We Have Heard on High
Joy to the World

Arr. by Phil Nitz

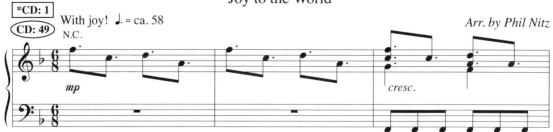

NARRATOR: It's Christmas! Ring the bells! Sound the trumpets!
Proclaim the glory of Christ who has come to dwell among His people.
This is the season to rejoice and what better way to celebrate than to sing!

1st time: Unison melody *(Sop. and Bass parts)*
2nd time: SATB
*"Sing, Sing, Sing"

Sing, sing, sing! This is a time___ for re-joic - ing!

Come, lift your voic - es and___ sing, sing,

sing! Join in the song___ of the sea - son!

Wor - ship Christ, the new - born King. Come and wor - ship.

Come and wor - ship. Wor - ship Christ, the new - born

King. Hark! the her - ald

*"Hark! the Herald Angels Sing"

CD: 3
CD: 51

47

an - gels   sing,_____   "Glo - ry   to   the   new - born   King!

50

Peace   on   earth,   and   mer - cy   mild–_____   God   and   sin - ners

53

rec - on - ciled."   Joy - ful,   all   ye   na - tions,   rise;_____

*"Angels We Have Heard on High"

new - born King."

Glo - - - ri - a in ex - cel - sis De - o!

(Without music)

NARRATOR: Long before the angel Gabriel's visit to Mary, God's people were already experiencing what it meant to live in expectation. *(Music begins)* The writings of the prophets would foreshadow the events to come even as the world longed for a Redeemer. Centuries of hope and wonder would pass as they waited for God to fulfill His covenant with Israel.

O Come, Emmanuel

with
O Come, O Come, Emmanuel

Words and Music by
PHIL MEHRENS and
NICK ROBERTSON
Arr. by Phil Nitz

PLEASE NOTE: The copying of this music is prohibited by law and is not covered by CCLI or OneLicense.net.

22

CD: 9
CD: 57

God, hear Your peo - ple as we pray. Come, O come, Em - man - u - el, God with us, will You come and dwell

CD: 10

CD: 58

26

CD: 12
CD: 60

*"O Come, O Come, Emmanuel"

30

31

113

man - u - el.

Em - man - u -

E

A²

A²

116

el.

E

E

E

8vb -

(Without music)

NARRATOR: The concept of hope is certainly not a new one nor
is it exclusive to believers alone. For some, it is merely a sense of
longing or a feeling of anticipation, but for the people of God it
represents the very foundation of our existence. Hope enables us
to live in the confidence that His word is true and He will not
forsake His own. And so it was, in the fullness of God's time,
beneath the stillness of a Bethlehem sky, the Hope of the World
was born. *(Music begins)* Scripture tells us they wrapped Him in
swaddling clothes, and laid Him in a manger; because there was
no room for them in the inn.

Hope for the World

Words and Music by
MICHAEL BOGGS, CHAD CATES
and TONY WOOD
Arr. by Phil Nitz

Lord, our long-ing hearts be-hold_____ the mir-a-cle the man-ger holds:_____ Hope_____ for the world,

34

40

47

Je - sus, Son of God, You are

Hope for the world.

(Without music)

NARRATOR: On the night Christ was born in Bethlehem, we tend to picture the event as one of peaceful serenity with a young mother cradling her newborn in her arms, but the scene could hardly have been more different on a nearby hillside where some shepherds stood watch over their sheep. An angel of the Lord appeared in the heavens with the announcement of the ages that Christ the Lord was born in the City of David. As amazing as that moment must have seemed for the nervous shepherds, they had no way of knowing church was just getting started. *(Music begins)* Suddenly the angel was joined by a multitude of heavenly host praising God, and saying, "Glory to God in the highest, and on earth peace, good will toward men."

Midnight Hallelujah

Words and Music by
DAVE CLARK and CLIFF DUREN
Arr. by Phil Nitz

56

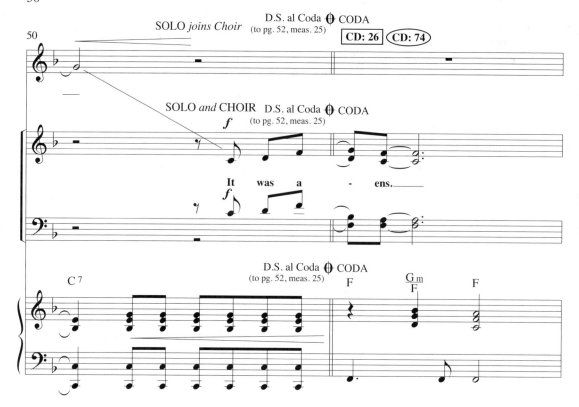

60

63

The Silent, Starry Night

Words and Music by
JOHN CHISUM and
PHIL MEHRENS
Arr. by Phil Nitz

*NARRATOR: For unto us a child is born, unto us a son is given: and the government shall be upon His shoulder: and His name shall be called Wonderful, Counselor, the mighty God, the everlasting Father, the Prince of Peace. Of the increase of His government and peace there shall be no end.

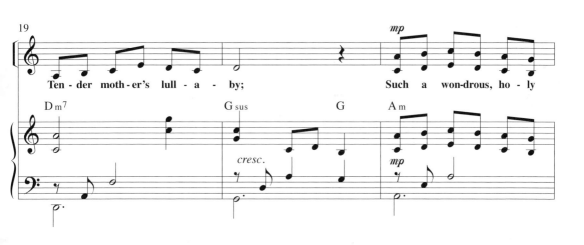

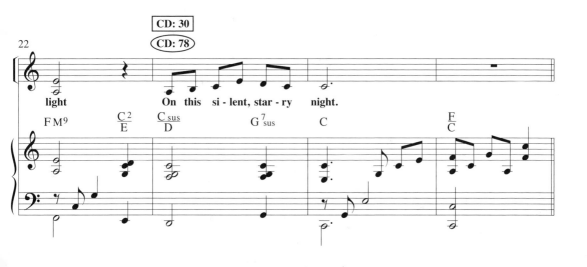

66

44

mf

us on this si - lent, star - ry night.

C 2/E   A m7   D m7   G sus   G 7sus   C

dim.   *mf*

CD: 32
CD: 80

47

F/C   D♭   G♭/D♭

50

mf

Sleep - ing cat - tle stand - ing by,   Vir - gin moth - er with her

mf

D♭   D♭   E♭m7

On this si - lent, star - ry night.

(Without music)

NARRATOR: 2000 years have come and gone since God sent His only Son that we might have life and have it more abundantly. We decorate the tree and add our voices to the carols of old, proudly proclaiming, "Joy to the world! The Lord is come!"

To those walking in darkness, He is light. To a people in despair, He is hope. *(Music begins)* The joy of the season is found in the good news of the gospel . . . Christ has come to seek and save that which was lost. And life as we knew it will never be the same . . . all because a Baby came.

Because a Baby Came

with
O Holy Night

Words and Music by
NICK ROBERTSON, ANNA CLARK
and ALISEN WELLS
Arr. by Phil Nitz

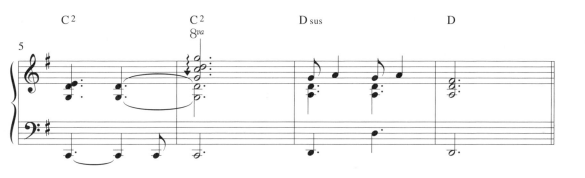

There, up in the night sky, a star Shone with a

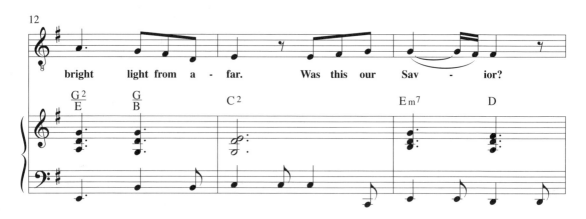

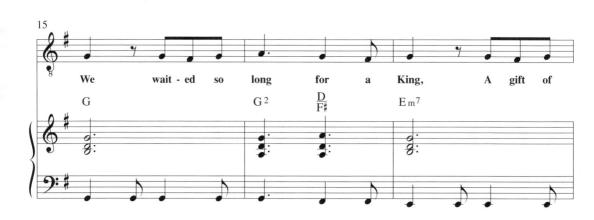

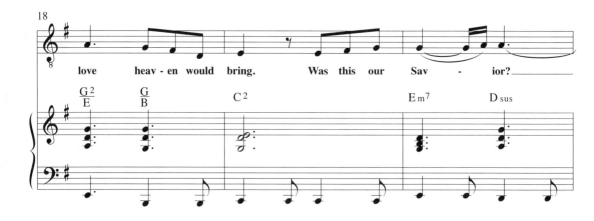

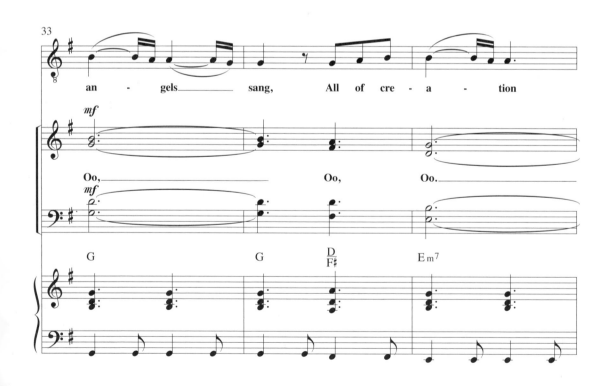

CD: 36

42 CD: 84

came.

came.

G   E m7   D   D sus   D   C 2

MALE SOLO
45   mf

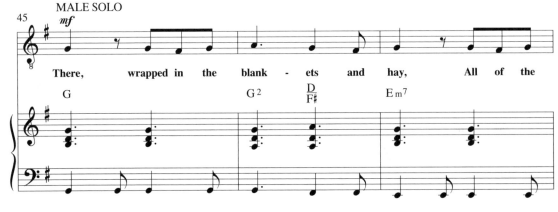

There,   wrapped in   the   blank - ets   and   hay,   All   of   the

G   G 2   D/F#   E m7

48

world   stood there   a - mazed   We   met   our   Sav - ior._____

G2/E   G/B   C 2   E m7   D sus

51

While the world was fast a - sleep,_____ The whole

CHOIR *unis.*
mf

While the world was fast a - sleep,
mf

D sus   D   A m⁷   G   D/F♯

CD: 37
CD: 85

54

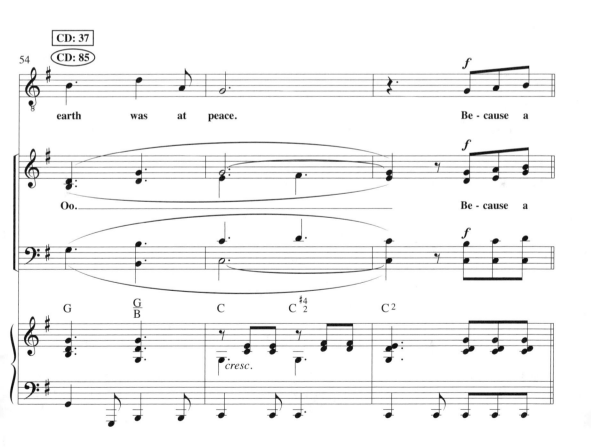

earth was at peace. Be - cause a

f

Oo._____ Be - cause a

f

G   G/B   C   C♯⁴₂   C²

cresc.

57

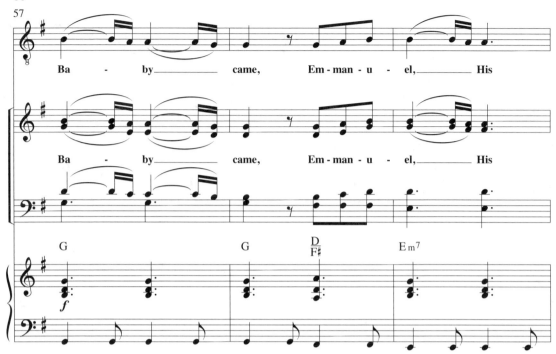

Ba - by _____ came, Em - man - u - el, _____ His

60

name, Born on that night, love mag - ni - fied. And then the

an - gels_____ sang, All of cre - a - tion

G G D/F# Em7

praised. Glo - ry on high, God heard our__ cry, We'll nev - er

Em7 G/B Am7 Em7

82

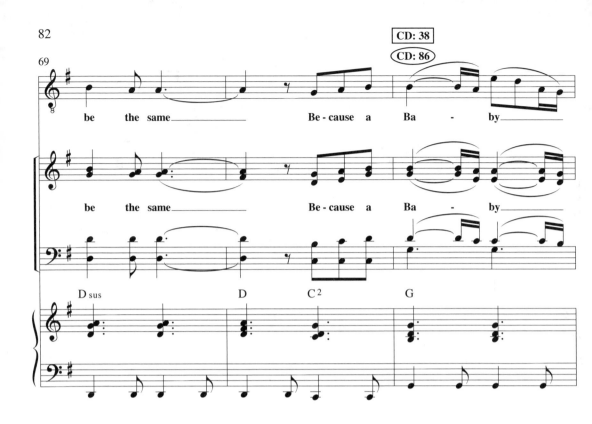

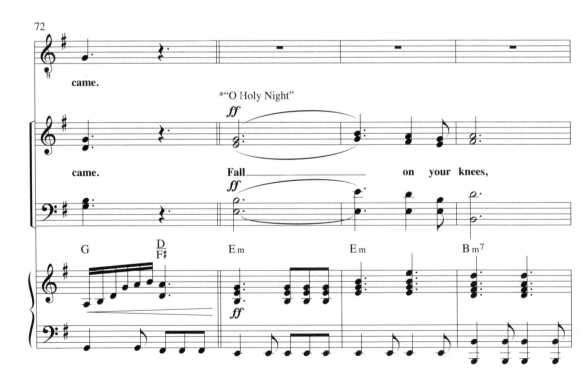

86

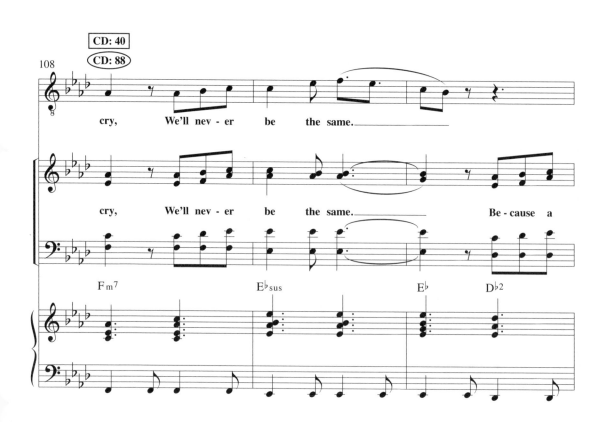

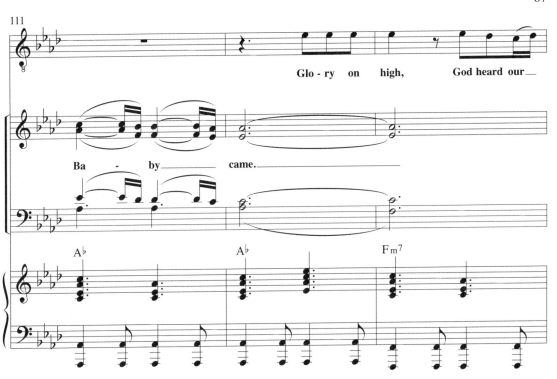

111

Glo - ry on high, God heard our

Ba - by came.

114

cry,

Born on that

Be - cause a Ba - by came.

(Without music)

NARRATOR: If we were to try and reduce the entire story of Christmas down to one word, it would have to be "love." For nothing short of love would compel a Father to give His only begotten Son, so that whoever believed in Him could live forever. Only love would permit a King to come as a pauper . . . to exchange the glory of heaven for the agony of a cross. *(Music begins)* Only love would look beyond who we have been and what we have done and see something worth redeeming . . . yes . . . love truly is the story of Christmas.

Let My Soul Sing (Gloria)

Words and Music by
MICHAEL FARREN, STUART GARRARD
and DUSTIN SMITH
Arr. by Phil Nitz

92

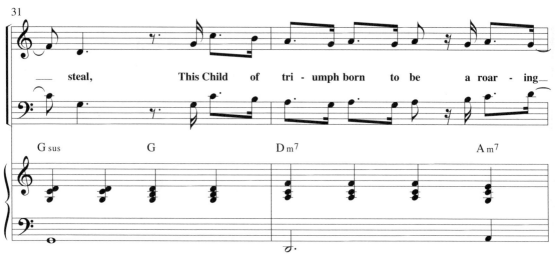

43
a.
Let my soul sing glo - ri - a, glo - ri -
C C/E G C/E F F G Am G/B
45
ff
a.
Let my soul sing glo - ri - a, glo - ri -
C C/E G C/E F F G Am G/B
47
a.
Let my soul sing glo - ri - a, glo - ri -
C C/E G C/E F F G Am G/B